# Building Shapes

**Susan Canizares**
**Samantha Berger**

**Scholastic Inc.**
**New York • Toronto • London • Auckland • Sydney**

**Acknowledgments**

**Literacy Specialist:** Linda Cornwell

**Learning Center Consultant:** Ellen Booth Church

**Design**: Silver Editions

**Photo Research:** Silver Editions

**Endnotes**: Susan Russell

**Endnote Illustrations**: Hokanson/Cichetti

---

Photographs:  Cover: Thomas Friedmann/Photo Researchers, Inc.; p. 1: Glen Allison/Tony Stone Images; p. 2: Stephen Johnson/Tony Stone Images; p. 3: David Ball/The Stock Market; p. 4: Michael Busselle/Tony Stone Images; p. 5: Thomas Friedmann/Photo Researchers, Inc.; p. 6: David R. Frazier/Photo Researchers, Inc.; p. 7: Spencer Grant/Gamma Liaison; p. 8: David Barnes/The Stock Market; p. 9: Hugh Sitton/Tony Stone Images; p. 10: (l) B & C Alexander/Photo Researchers, Inc.; (r): Michele Burgess/The Stock Market; p. 11: (l) Lou Renault/Photo Researchers, Inc.; (r): Steve Elmore/Tony Stone Images; p. 12: Vic Bider/Photo Edit.

6   7   8   9   10       08       03

Buildings are many shapes.

▲ Buildings are triangles.

 Buildings are squares.

● Buildings are circles.

Buildings are rectangles.

Buildings are triangles, squares,

circles, and rectangles.

A building can even be a pentagon!

# Building Shapes

Buildings can be many shapes. The Chicago skyline shows many of them: squares, triangles, rectangles — even a diamond! These different flat shapes form the sides of the buildings. When the sides are put together, they form a three-dimensional structure. For example, triangles form a pyramid and squares form a cube. The shape of a building often depends on what the building will be used for and where it is located. When architects design buildings, they must also think about what shapes and sizes will look best in the environment.

**Triangles** Triangles that are put together form pyramids. Triangles are the most stable shape to build with because they are very hard to knock down. This glass pyramid is part of the Louvre Museum in Paris. It isn't meant to be lived in, just looked at!

The enormous pyramids at Giza in Egypt weren't meant to be lived in either. They were built by the Egyptians thousands of years ago to hold the bodies of their kings, the pharaohs. They are almost solid stone with small burial chambers inside.

**Squares** A square is one of the most common shapes for a building. It has lots of inside space and makes a good shape for a house. Often such structures are designed to be just the right size for one family. This building is a farmhouse in Provence, France.

This apartment complex is in Montreal, Canada. It is made up of a lot of squares stacked together. This is a place where many families can live — each family has its own square home!

**Circles** Buildings that are circles have special uses. A circle is a good shape for a stadium because people can be seated all around on the sloping sides and see the game on the field below. This is the Bush Stadium in St. Louis, Missouri.

Another famous circular building is the Guggenheim Museum in New York City. There is a spiral walkway that goes along the inside of the building. People stroll along this walkway to view the artwork on display.

**Rectangles** The famous Falling Water house in Pennsylvania was designed by the architect Frank Lloyd Wright. It is made up of many rectangles fitted together and is actually built on top of a waterfall!

The rectangle is the shape used for most of the tall buildings in cities—especially office buildings, which can hold many people in a relatively small space. Often these tall office buildings are in the same neighborhood. They form the business district of a city. This is the business district of Singapore.

**Triangles, squares, circles, and rectangles** Tents all over the world have triangular shapes. This one is a sheepherder's tent in Norway. When a builder uses logs that are all the same length, it results in a square building. This is a square log cabin in Alaska. One of the oldest round buildings in the world is the Coliseum in Rome. It is an arena and was used long ago for celebrations and games.
The two rectangles here are the famous World Trade Center twin towers in New York. They are the tallest skyscrapers in the city.

**Pentagon** There is one famous building that isn't a triangle or square, circle or rectangle — it's a pentagon shape. That means it has five sides. This is the huge building called the Pentagon that houses the Defense Department of the United States Government.